Investing for Beginners: A guide to understanding basic investment concepts, including stocks, bonds, mutual funds, and ETFs.

Allen E. Henley

All rights reserved no part of this publication may be reproduced, distributed, or transmitted in any form or by any means including photocopying, recording or other electronic or mechanical methods, without the prior written permission of the publisher, except in the case of brief quotations embodied in critical reviews and certain other noncommercial uses permitted by the copyright law.

Copyright ©

YOUR FREE GIFT

Thank you for purchasing my book!

To show my gratitude, I would love to send you a **FREE BONUS BOOK**,which contains 3 chapters.

●**Best Resources and Tools for Investors**(my favorite tool and one which I *highly* recommend for a beginner)
●**Investment Strategies & Tips**

●**5 Common Investment Mistakes And How To Avoid Them As a Beginner**

TABLE OF CONTENTS:

INTRODUCTION

CHAPTER 1:
IMPORTANCE OF INVESTING
CHAPTER 2:
STOCKS- THE BUILDING BLOCKS OF WEALTH
CHAPTER 3:
BONDS-THE SAFE HAVENS OF INVESTING
CHAPTER 4.
MUTUAL FUNDS - POOLING RESOURCES FOR GREATER GAINS
CHAPTER 5.
ETFs - THE VERSATILE INVESTMENT VEHICLE
CONCLUSION
YOUR FREE GIFT.

INTRODUCTION

Let's break down what investing really means. Picture this: you've got some extra money, and instead of letting it sit around doing nothing, you decide to put it to work. That's essentially what investing is all about—using your money to make more money.

When you invest, you're buying assets like stocks, bonds, mutual funds, or real estate. These assets have the potential to grow in value over time or provide you with income, like dividends from stocks or interest from bonds. Think of it as planting seeds. Each investment is a seed that, with the right care and conditions, can grow and multiply, giving you a bigger harvest in the future.

Another cool thing about investing is that it helps you beat inflation. Inflation is like a sneaky thief that erodes your money's value over time. By investing, you can earn returns that outpace inflation, ensuring your money keeps its purchasing power.

Now, I won't sugarcoat it—investing does come with risks. The value of your investments can go up and down. But don't let that scare you. There are ways to manage risk, like diversifying your investments (spreading your money across different types of assets) and investing for the long term.

So, in a nutshell, investing is putting your money to work to grow over time. It's about making smart choices today to secure your financial future.

CHAPTER 1:
IMPORTANCE OF INVESTING

Let's talk about why investing is so crucial. Imagine you're sitting on a bit of money. Maybe it's just sitting in a savings account, earning next to nothing in interest. That's where investing comes in—it's like giving your money a job to do, a way to grow over time and help you achieve your financial goals.

First off, there's this amazing concept called compound interest. It's pretty much magic. When you invest, not only do you earn money on your initial investment, but you also earn money on the interest that accumulates. Over time, this can turn a small amount into a significant sum. Think of it as planting a tree;

initially, it's small, but given time, water, and care, it grows and bears fruit.

Why is this important? Because life is expensive, and there are things you'll want or need money for in the future—buying a house, starting a business, traveling the world, or even just retiring comfortably. If you rely solely on savings, you might find it challenging to meet these goals. Investing allows your money to work harder for you, so you can reach these milestones more easily.

Then there's the whole idea of beating inflation. Inflation is the gradual increase in prices over time, meaning your money loses purchasing power if it just sits around. By investing, you can potentially earn returns that outpace inflation, ensuring your money retains its value and grows.

Now, I know what you might be thinking—investing sounds risky. And you're right; there is some risk involved. But remember, there's a balance between risk and return. The key is to find a risk level you're comfortable with and diversify your investments. That way, if one investment doesn't perform well, others might, balancing things out.

In essence, investing is all about preparing for the future. It's like planting seeds today so you can enjoy a lush garden tomorrow. It might seem daunting at first, but with a bit of knowledge and careful planning, you can turn your financial dreams into reality. And hey, I'm here to help you every step of the way.

SETTING FINANCIAL GOALS

Think of financial goals as the roadmap to your dream life. Without them, it's like embarking on a road trip with no destination in mind. Sure, you might have fun along the way, but you'll likely end up lost and frustrated.

Firstly, you need to figure out what you want. What does your dream life look like? Maybe it's buying a cozy home, traveling to exotic places, starting your own business, or retiring early. Whatever it is, jot it down. Don't worry about the details just yet—this is all about dreaming big.

Now, let's break those dreams down into specific, measurable goals. For example, instead of saying, "I want to save money," say, "I want to save $20,000 for a down payment on a house in three years." The more specific you are, the better. This way, you have a clear target to aim for.

Next, prioritize your goals. Some might be short-term, like saving for a vacation next year, while others are long-term, like building a retirement nest egg. It's important to balance these. You don't want to focus solely on the future and miss out on enjoying the present. So, think about what's most important to you right now and what can wait a little longer.

Once you've got your goals sorted out, it's time to make a plan. This is where things get a bit more practical. Start by looking at your current financial situation—how much you earn, how much you spend, and how much you can realistically save or invest each month. Then, map out a strategy to reach each goal. For example, if you need to save $20,000 in three years, you'd need to save around $555 a month. Can you swing that? If not, where can you cut back or how can you earn a little extra?

Don't forget to track your progress. Set milestones and celebrate when you reach them. This not only keeps you motivated but also helps you see if you need to adjust your plan. Life happens, and sometimes goals need to shift.

That's totally okay. The key is to stay flexible and keep your eyes on the prize.

Lastly, remember to enjoy the journey. Setting and working towards financial goals isn't just about the end result. It's about building good habits, learning, and growing along the way. Plus, it feels pretty amazing to see your hard work pay off.

RISK AND RETURN

Let's get into something that's at the heart of investing: **risk and return**. Understanding this concept is like learning the rules of a game. Once you get it, you're much better equipped to play—and win.

First, let's talk about **return**. When we say "return," we're talking about the money you earn from your investments. This could be through capital gains (when the value of what you own goes up) or through income, like dividends from stocks or interest from bonds. Simply put, return is the reward you get for investing your money.

Now, here's the kicker—there's no such thing as a free lunch. **Risk** is the uncertainty or the potential for loss in your investments. Every investment carries some degree of risk, which means there's always a chance you might not get back what you put in. But don't let this scare you off; risk is a normal part of investing.

Here's where things get interesting: **risk and return** are closely related. Generally speaking, the higher the potential return, the higher the risk. Think of it like this: if you want a big reward, you have to be willing to take on more risk. It's like climbing a mountain—the higher you go, the better the view, but the climb gets steeper and more challenging.

On the flip side, lower-risk investments tend to offer lower returns. These are like the gentle hills of the investment world. They're easier to climb, but the view isn't as spectacular. For example, government bonds are considered low-risk because they're backed by the government, but they also offer lower returns compared to stocks.

So, how do you balance risk and return? It's all about finding what works for you. This involves considering your risk tolerance, which is basically how much risk you're comfortable taking on. Some people are okay with the ups and downs of high-risk investments because they're aiming for higher returns. Others prefer a more steady and predictable approach.

- **Here's a tip:** diversify your investments. By spreading your money across different types of assets (like stocks, bonds, mutual funds, and ETFs), you can manage risk better. If one investment doesn't perform well, others might do better, balancing things out. It's like not putting all your eggs in one basket.

Also, think about your time horizon—how long you plan to invest before you need the money. If you're investing for the long term, you might be able to take on more risk because you have time to ride out the market's ups and downs. For short-term goals, lower-risk investments might be more appropriate.

In a nutshell, understanding risk and return helps you make smarter investment choices. It's about weighing the potential rewards against the potential risks and finding a balance that suits your financial goals and comfort level.

CHAPTER 2:

STOCKS- THE BUILDING BLOCKS OF WEALTH

WHAT ARE STOCKS:. Think of stocks as your ticket to owning a piece of a company. When you buy a stock, you're essentially buying a small slice of that company and becoming a shareholder. Sounds cool, right?

Here's how it works: companies issue stocks to raise money for various things like expanding their business, launching new products, or paying off debt. In return, they offer investors like you a chance to share in their profits and growth. If the company does well, the value of your stock goes up, and you can sell it for a profit. Plus, some companies pay dividends, which are regular cash payments to shareholders.

Stocks come in two main flavors: **common stocks** and **preferred stocks**. Common stocks are the most common type (no pun intended). They give you voting rights at shareholder meetings and a share of the company's profits through dividends and capital gains. Preferred stocks, on the other hand, usually don't come with voting rights, but they offer fixed dividends and have a higher claim on assets if the company goes bankrupt.

The stock market is where all the action happens. This is where buyers and sellers come together to trade stocks. You've probably heard of major stock exchanges like the New York Stock Exchange (NYSE) or NASDAQ. These are the marketplaces where stocks are bought and sold. The prices of stocks on these exchanges can change constantly based on supply and demand, company performance, and broader economic factors.

Investing in stocks can be incredibly rewarding, but it's important to understand that it comes with risks. Stock prices can be volatile, meaning they can go up and down quickly. One day you might see your investment soaring, and the next, it might take a dip. This is why it's essential to do your homework before investing. Look at a company's financial health, its industry, and future growth potential. This is called fundamental analysis.

There's also another approach called technical analysis, where you look at stock price charts and trends to make investment decisions. Some people swear by it, while others prefer sticking to fundamentals. It's all about finding what works best for you.

Diversification is your friend when it comes to stocks. Instead of putting all your money into one company's stock, spread it out across different companies, industries, and even regions. This way, if one stock doesn't perform well, others in your portfolio might balance things out.

Remember, investing in stocks is a long-term game. Sure, some people make money trading stocks frequently, but for most of us, it's about buying quality stocks and holding onto them for a while to let their value grow. Patience and

HERE'S HOW THE STOCK MARKET WORKS

Think of the stock market as a bustling marketplace, but instead of fruits and veggies, you're buying and selling ownership in companies. It's where all the action happens when it comes to trading stocks.

So, here's the basics: the stock market is made up of various stock exchanges, like the New York Stock Exchange (NYSE) and NASDAQ. These exchanges are platforms where buyers and sellers meet to trade stocks. Just like any marketplace, prices are determined by supply and demand. If lots of people want to buy a stock, its price goes up. If lots of people want to sell, the price goes down.

When a company wants to raise money, it can issue stocks in an initial public offering (IPO). This is when the company sells shares to the public for the first time. Once the IPO is done, those shares can be traded on the stock market.

Every trade that happens on the stock market is facilitated by stockbrokers. These are professionals or platforms that help you buy and sell stocks. You can think of them as the middlemen. Nowadays, thanks to online brokers, you can buy and sell stocks with just a few clicks on your computer or smartphone.

The stock market is influenced by a variety of factors. Company performance is a big one. If a company reports strong earnings or announces a new product, its stock price might go up.

Conversely, if it has a bad quarter or faces a scandal, its stock price might drop. Then there's the economy as a whole. Economic indicators like unemployment rates, inflation, and interest rates can impact the market. When the economy is doing well, the stock market generally performs better.

Another key player in the stock market is the investor sentiment. This is basically how investors feel about the market. If investors are optimistic, they buy more stocks, driving prices up. If they're pessimistic, they sell, driving prices down. News and events can heavily influence sentiment. For example, political events, natural disasters, or major technological breakthroughs can cause market swings.

One cool thing about the stock market is the variety of ways you can invest. You can buy individual stocks if you believe in specific companies. Or, you can invest in mutual funds or ETFs, which are like baskets of stocks. These are great for diversification because they spread your investment across many different companies, reducing your risk.

Understanding how to read stock market data is also important. When you look at a stock quote, you'll see things like the current price, the day's high and low prices, the 52-week high and low, the volume of shares traded, and more. This information helps you make informed decisions about when to buy or sell.

There's also the concept of market indices, like the S&P 500 or the Dow Jones Industrial Average. These indices track the performance of a group of stocks and give you a snapshot of how the market, or a segment of it, is doing overall. When people say "the market is up," they're usually referring to these indices going up.

In summary, the stock market is a dynamic and exciting place where fortunes can be made and lost. It's driven by supply and demand, influenced by a myriad of factors, and offers numerous ways to invest. By understanding how it works, you're better equipped to navigate it and make smart investment decisions.

HOW TO GET STARTED WITH STOCKS

It might seem a bit overwhelming at first, but trust me, once you get the hang of it, it's pretty exciting. Here's a *step-by-step* guide to help you get started.

1. Set Your Goals and Determine Your Risk Tolerance

First things first, figure out what you want to achieve with your investments. Are you saving for retirement, a down payment on a house, or maybe just looking to grow your wealth over time? Knowing your goals will help you make better investment choices.

Next, think about your risk tolerance—**how much risk are you comfortable with**? Stocks can be volatile, meaning their prices can go up and down a lot. If you're okay with that and looking for higher returns, you might go for more aggressive investments. If you prefer stability, you might choose more conservative options.

2. **Learn the Basics**

Before you start investing, it's essential to understand some basic concepts. Learn about different types of stocks (common vs. preferred), how dividends work, and what affects stock prices. There are tons of resources online, including articles, videos, and courses, to get you up to speed.

3. **Choose a Brokerage Account:** To buy and sell stocks, you'll need a brokerage account. This is like a bank account but for investments. There are many online brokers to choose from, like Robinhood, E*TRADE, and TD Ameritrade. Look for one with low fees, a user-friendly platform, and good customer service.

4. **Fund Your Account**

Once you've chosen a brokerage, you'll need to fund your account. This means transferring money from your bank account to your brokerage account. Most brokers have a minimum deposit requirement, so make sure you're aware of that.

5. **Start with Research**

Before you buy your first stock, do some research. Look at companies you're interested in and check their financial health, performance history, and future growth potential. You can use financial news websites, company annual reports, and stock analysis tools to gather information.

6. Make Your First Purchase

Ready to buy? Log into your brokerage account, search for the stock you want to purchase by its ticker symbol (e.g., AAPL for Apple), and place your order. You can choose between different order types, like market orders (buy at the current price) or limit orders (buy only if the stock hits a certain price).

7. Diversify Your Portfolio

To manage risk, don't put all your money into one stock. Diversify your investments across different sectors and industries. You can also consider investing in mutual funds or ETFs, which are collections of stocks and provide instant diversification.

8. Monitor Your Investments

Keep an eye on your investments, but don't get too obsessed with daily price movements. Stocks can be volatile, and it's normal for prices to fluctuate. Focus on the long-term performance and make adjustments to your portfolio as needed.

9. Stay Informed and Keep Learning

The stock market is always changing, so it's important to stay informed. Follow financial news, read books on investing, and consider joining investment forums or groups to learn from others. The more you know, the better your investment decisions will be.

10. Be Patient and Stay Disciplined

Investing in stocks is a marathon, not a sprint. It's important to be patient and stay disciplined, even during market downturns. Stick to your investment plan and avoid making impulsive decisions based on short-term market movements.

So, there you have it—a beginner's guide to getting started with stocks. It might seem like a lot at first, but take it step by step, and soon you'll feel more confident in your investing journey. Let's get started and watch your investments grow!

CHAPTER 3:

BONDS-THE SAFE HAVENS OF INVESTING

UNDERSTANDING BONDS

If stocks are like owning a piece of a company, bonds are like giving a company or government a loan. When you buy a bond, you're lending your money to the issuer (the company or government), and in return, they promise to pay you back with interest. It's a bit like being the bank!

Here's how it works: when you purchase a bond, you're essentially agreeing to lend your money for a set period, called the maturity date. During this time, the issuer pays you interest, usually twice a year. When the bond reaches maturity, they return your initial investment, also known as the principal.

There are a few different *types of bonds* you should know about:

1. Government Bonds: Issued by national governments. In the U.S., these are called Treasury bonds. They're considered very safe because they're backed by the government.

2. Municipal Bonds: Issued by states, cities, or other local governments. They're often used to fund public projects like roads and schools. The cool thing about "munis" is that the interest you earn is often tax-free.

3. Corporate Bonds: Issued by companies. These usually offer higher interest rates than government bonds because they come with a bit more risk. The riskier the company, the higher the interest rate they have to offer to attract investors.

4.Savings Bonds: Issued by the government as a low-risk, low-return investment, usually aimed at individual investors. They're a great way to save over a long period.

●**Why Invest in Bonds?**
Bonds are generally considered safer than stocks because you're more likely to get your initial investment back, along with interest. They're a great way to diversify your portfolio and reduce overall risk. Think of them as the stabilizers in your investment mix.

●**Understanding Bond Yields**
The interest rate you earn from a bond is called the yield. There are a couple of ways to look at this:

1.Coupon Rate: The fixed interest rate the bond pays based on its face value. For example, if you have a $1,000 bond with a 5% coupon rate, you'll get $50 a year in interest.

2.Current Yield: This is the bond's annual interest payment divided by its current price. Bond prices can fluctuate, so the current yield gives you a sense of what you're earning based on the market price.

- **Risks of Investing in Bonds**

While bonds are generally safer than stocks, they're not risk-free. Here are a few things to watch out for:

1.Interest Rate Risk: When interest rates rise, bond prices usually fall. This is because new bonds are issued with higher yields, making older bonds less attractive.

2.Credit Risk: This is the risk that the issuer might default and be unable to pay back the bond. Government bonds are low-risk in this regard, but corporate bonds can vary depending on the company's financial health.

3.Inflation Risk: If inflation rises faster than the bond's interest rate, your purchasing power could be eroded. Essentially, you might not be earning enough to keep up with rising prices.

- **Buying and Selling Bonds**

You can buy bonds through a brokerage, just like stocks. Some bonds are sold directly by the government or issuing companies. You can hold a bond until it matures or sell it before then. The price you get for selling it will depend on current interest rates and the bond's credit quality.

- **Balancing Your Portfolio**

Bonds are a key part of a balanced investment portfolio. They provide steady income and can help cushion against the volatility of stocks. The right mix of stocks and bonds depends on your financial goals, risk tolerance, and investment horizon.

So, that's the lowdown on bonds. They're a solid way to earn steady returns and diversify your investments. Ready to add some bonds to your portfolio? Let's do this and make your investments even stronger!

HOW BONDS ARE PRICED

This might sound a bit technical, but I promise to break it down in a way that makes sense. Knowing how bond pricing works can help you make better investment decisions.

- **Face Value and Price**

First, let's get some terminology straight. The face value (or par value) of a bond is the amount you'll get back when the bond matures. It's usually $1,000 per bond for corporate bonds, but it can vary. However, the price you pay for a bond might be different from its face value. It can be more (a premium) or less (a discount), depending on various factors.

•Interest Rates and Bond Prices

One of the biggest factors affecting bond prices is interest rates. There's an inverse relationship between bond prices and interest rates. When interest rates rise, bond prices fall. When interest rates fall, bond prices rise. Here's why:

Imagine you have a bond with a 5% coupon rate, meaning it pays $50 a year in interest on a $1,000 face value. If interest rates rise to 6%, new bonds are being issued that pay $60 a year. Your bond, which pays only $50, isn't as attractive anymore. To sell it, you'd have to lower the price, so the yield matches the new 6% rate.

•Calculating Bond Prices

Bond prices are typically quoted as a percentage of their face value. If a bond is trading at 102, it's selling for 102% of its face value, or $1,020. If it's trading at 98, it's selling for 98% of its face value, or $980.

To get a bit more technical, bond prices are influenced by the present value of its future cash flows. This includes the interest payments (coupons) and the repayment of the face value at maturity. Investors discount these future cash flows back to their present value using the current market interest rate. The sum of these present values is the bond's price.

- **Yield and Bond Pricing**

The yield of a bond is another crucial aspect of its pricing. There are different types of yields to understand:

- **Coupon Yield:** This is the bond's annual interest payment divided by its face value. For example, a $1,000 bond with a $50 annual coupon payment has a 5% coupon yield.

●**Current Yield:** This is the bond's annual interest payment divided by its current price. If that same bond is selling for $900, its current yield is about 5.56% ($50 ÷ $900).

Yield to Maturity (YTM): This is the total return expected on a bond if held until maturity. It considers the bond's current market price, its face value, the coupon interest rate, and the time to maturity. YTM is a bit more complex to calculate, but most financial websites and tools will do it for you.

●**Market Conditions and Bond Prices**

Other factors can influence bond prices, too. For example:

●**Credit Quality:** Bonds issued by entities with strong financial health (like the U.S. government or blue-chip companies) are generally more stable and lower-risk. If a company's credit rating is downgraded, its bond prices might drop because of the perceived higher risk.

- **Inflation: Higher:** inflation erodes the purchasing power of future cash flows, making bonds less attractive, which can drive prices down.

- **Supply and Demand:** Like any market, bond prices are influenced by supply and demand. If more people want to buy bonds than sell them, prices go up, and vice versa.

- **Buying and Selling Bonds**

When you buy a bond in the secondary market, you might pay more or less than its face value, depending on the current interest rates and other factors we've discussed. The price you pay will determine your yield, which is why understanding bond pricing is so important.

INVESTING IN BONDS

Let me show you a *step-by-step* guide to get you started:

1. Determine Your Investment Goals
Before you invest, think about what you want to achieve. Are you looking for regular , preserving your capital, or balancing your portfolio? Your goals will help determine which types of bonds are right for you.

2. Understand Your Risk Tolerance
Different bonds come with different levels of risk. Government bonds are usually safer, while corporate bonds can offer higher returns with higher risk. Assess how much risk you're comfortable with.

3. Choose How to Buy Bonds
You can buy bonds directly or invest in bond funds. Here are your options:

- **Individual Bonds:** You can buy them directly through a brokerage account. This allows you to pick specific bonds, but it requires more research and knowledge.

- **Bond Funds:** These are mutual funds or exchange-traded funds (ETFs) that invest in a variety of bonds. They offer diversification and professional management, making them a good option for beginners.

4. Research and Select Bonds

If you're buying individual bonds, research the issuers' credit ratings and financial health. Ratings agencies like Moody's, S&P, and Fitch provide ratings that indicate the issuer's credit quality. Look for bonds with higher ratings if you want lower risk.

5. Diversify Your Bond Investments

Just like with stocks, diversification is key. Spread your investments across different types of bonds and issuers to reduce risk. This way, if one bond underperforms, others in your portfolio can help balance it out.

6. Monitor Your Investments
Keep an eye on your bond investments, but don't stress over daily fluctuations. Bonds are typically long-term investments, and their prices are less volatile than stocks. Focus on the overall performance and adjust your portfolio as needed to stay aligned with your goals.

Benefits of Bond Investing
- **Steady Income:** Bonds provide regular interest payments, which can be a reliable source of income.
- **Capital Preservation:** Bonds are less risky than stocks, helping to preserve your initial investment.
- **Diversification:** Including bonds in your portfolio can reduce overall risk and volatility.

Investing in bonds can be a great way to add stability and income to your investment portfolio. By understanding the different types of bonds, determining your investment goals, and diversifying your investments, you'll be well on your way to making smart bond investment choices.

CHAPTER 4.

MUTUAL FUNDS - POOLING RESOURCES FOR GREATER GAINS

WHAT ARE MUTUAL FUNDS?

Imagine you want to invest in a bunch of different stocks, bonds, or other assets, but you don't have the time or knowledge to pick them yourself. This is where mutual funds come in handy.

What Is a Mutual Fund?

A mutual fund is like a big pot where a bunch of investors pool their money together. This pooled money is then used to buy a diversified portfolio of stocks, bonds, or other securities. The fund is managed by professional money managers who do all the research, buying, and selling for you.

Essentially, you're buying a piece of this big pot, which means you own a slice of all the investments within the fund.

How Mutual Funds Work?

Here's the basic idea:

1. You Invest: You put your money into the mutual fund by buying shares of the fund.

2. Pooling Money: Your money is combined with money from other investors.

3. Professional Management: Fund managers use this pooled money to buy a diversified portfolio of assets.

4. Earnings and Growth: As the assets in the portfolio grow or generate income (like dividends or interest), you earn a return based on your share of the fund.

5. NAV (Net Asset Value): The value of each share you own in the mutual fund is called the NAV, which is calculated daily based on the total value of the fund's assets divided by the number of shares.

Types of Mutual Funds

There are several types of mutual funds, each with different investment goals and strategies:

1. Stock (Equity) Funds: Invest mainly in stocks. They can be further divided into categories like growth funds, value funds, and sector funds.

2. Bond (Fixed-Income) Funds: Invest in bonds and other fixed-income securities. These funds aim to provide regular income with lower risk than stock funds.

3. Money Market Funds: Invest in short-term, low-risk securities. They aim to provide safety and liquidity with modest returns.

4. Balanced (Hybrid) Funds: Invest in a mix of stocks, bonds, and other assets to provide a balance of growth and income.

5.Index Funds: Track a specific market index, like the S&P 500. These funds aim to match the performance of the index they track and typically have lower fees.

6.Target-Date Funds: Designed for retirement investing, these funds automatically adjust their asset mix as you approach a target retirement date.

Costs of Mutual Funds

While mutual funds offer many benefits, they also come with costs:

- **Expense Ratios:** This is the annual fee that covers the fund's operating expenses, including the manager's fees. It's expressed as a percentage of the fund's assets.
- **Load Fees:** Some funds charge a fee when you buy (front-end load) or sell (back-end load) shares. Look for no-load funds to avoid these fees.

- **Other Fees:** There may be additional fees for things like account maintenance or trading within the fund.

How to Choose a Mutual Fund

When picking a mutual fund, consider these factors:

1. Investment Goals: What are you trying to achieve—growth, income, or a mix of both? Choose a fund that aligns with your goals.

2. Risk Tolerance: Different funds have different levels of risk. Make sure the fund matches your comfort level with risk.

3. Performance: Look at the fund's historical performance, but remember that past performance doesn't guarantee future results.

4.Fees: Compare expense ratios and other fees. Lower fees can mean more of your money stays invested and working for you.

5.Fund Manager: Research the fund manager's track record and investment style. A good manager can make a significant difference.

BENEFITS OF MUTUAL FUNDS

This why mutual funds are such a popular choice for investors. If you're looking for a simple, diversified, and professionally managed way to grow your money, mutual funds have a lot to offer. Here's a rundown of the key benefits:

1. Diversification: One of the biggest advantages of mutual funds is diversification. Imagine trying to buy a little bit of hundreds of different stocks and bonds on your own—that would be complicated and expensive. Mutual funds pool money from many investors, allowing you to own a small piece of a large and diverse portfolio. This helps spread out risk because if one investment in the fund underperforms, others might do well and balance it out.

2. Professional Management: Managing a diverse investment portfolio can be time-consuming and requires a lot of expertise. When you invest in a mutual fund, you're essentially hiring a professional fund manager to handle all the research, buying, and selling for you. These managers have the knowledge and resources to make informed investment decisions, aiming to achieve the best possible returns.

3. Accessibility: You don't need a lot of money to start investing in mutual funds. Many funds have low minimum investment requirements, making them accessible to almost anyone. This is great if you're just starting out and don't have a large amount of capital to invest.

4. Liquidity: Mutual funds are typically very liquid, meaning you can buy and sell your shares easily. Most mutual funds allow you to redeem your shares at the end of any trading day at the fund's current net asset value (NAV). This gives you the flexibility to access your money when you need it.

5. Variety of Choices: There are thousands of mutual funds out there, covering a wide range of investment styles and asset classes. Whether you're looking for aggressive growth, steady income, or a balanced approach, there's likely a mutual fund that fits your needs. You can invest in stock funds, bond funds, money market funds, index funds, sector funds, and more.

6. Convenience: Investing in mutual funds is convenient. You can set up automatic investments, reinvest dividends, and access a wide array of funds through a single brokerage account. Many brokers and fund companies offer tools and resources to help you choose and manage your investments easily.

7.Reinvestment of Income: Mutual funds often give you the option to automatically reinvest any income they generate, such as dividends and capital gains distributions. This can help compound your returns over time, as the reinvested amounts start to earn returns as well.

8.Economies of Scale: Because mutual funds pool money from many investors, they can benefit from economies of scale. This means they can buy and sell securities at lower transaction costs compared to individual investors. These savings can be passed on to investors in the form of lower fees and expenses.

9.Regulation and Transparency: Mutual funds are regulated by government agencies like the Securities and Exchange Commission (SEC) in the United States. This regulation helps ensure that mutual funds operate in the best interests of their investors. Funds are also required to provide regular reports and disclose important information, which helps you stay informed about your investment.

10. Tax Efficiency: Some mutual funds, particularly index funds and tax-managed funds, are designed to be tax-efficient. They aim to minimize taxable events, such as the sale of securities, which can help reduce your tax liability.

11. Automatic Rebalancing: Many mutual funds, especially target-date funds and balanced funds, automatically rebalance their portfolios. This means they adjust the allocation of assets to maintain a desired risk level or investment strategy. It saves you the hassle of doing it yourself and ensures your portfolio stays aligned with your investment goals.

The many benefits of mutual funds. They offer a convenient, diversified, and professionally managed way to invest your money, making them a great option whether you're just starting out or looking to add to your existing portfolio.

RISK OF MUTUAL FUNDS

While mutual funds have a lot of benefits, it's also important to understand the risks involved. No investment is without risk, and mutual funds are no exception. Let's talk about some of the key risks you should be aware of, with some examples to make it clearer.

1.Market Risk: Market risk, also known as *systematic risk*, is the risk that the value of your investments will fluctuate due to changes in the overall market. This can be caused by economic changes, political events, or other factors that affect the financial markets.

•*Example:*If you invest in a mutual fund that holds a lot of tech stocks, and there's a market-wide sell-off in tech due to regulatory changes, the value of your mutual fund could drop even if the individual companies in the fund are still doing well.

2.Interest Rate Risk: Interest rate risk is particularly relevant for bond funds. When interest rates rise, the value of existing bonds typically falls because new bonds are issued at higher rates.

•*Example:* Imagine you hold shares in a bond mutual fund, and the Federal Reserve decides to increase interest rates. The bonds your fund holds will likely decrease in value because new bonds will offer higher interest rates, making your existing bonds less attractive.

3.Credit Risk: Credit risk, or default risk, is the risk that a bond issuer will fail to make the required interest payments or repay the principal at maturity.

•*Example:* If your mutual fund includes bonds from a corporation that suddenly goes bankrupt, the bonds might default, leading to a loss in your fund's value.

4.Inflation Risk: Inflation risk is the danger that the purchasing power of your investment returns will be eroded by inflation.

•*Example:* If you have a mutual fund that invests in long-term bonds yielding 3%, but inflation rises to 4%, your real return is negative because the cost of goods and services is increasing faster than your returns.

5.Manager Risk: Mutual funds are managed by professional fund managers who make the decisions about which securities to buy and sell. Manager risk is the risk that the fund manager's decisions will not result in good performance.

•*Example:* If a new fund manager takes over your mutual fund and starts making poor investment choices or strays from the fund's original strategy, the fund's performance could suffer.

6. Liquidity Risk: Liquidity risk is the risk that you won't be able to sell your investment quickly enough or at a fair price.

•*Example:* Some mutual funds invest in less liquid assets, like real estate or certain types of bonds. If you need to sell your shares in a hurry, the fund might have to sell these assets at a lower price, potentially reducing your returns.

7. Expense Risk: Mutual funds charge fees and expenses that can eat into your returns.

•*Example:* If you invest in a mutual fund with a high expense ratio, like 2%, and it only returns 5% a year, your net return is only 3%. Over time, high fees can significantly reduce your investment gains.

8. Currency Risk: If you invest in mutual funds that hold foreign investments, currency risk comes into play.

•*Example:* Suppose you invest in an international mutual fund that holds European stocks. If the euro weakens against the U.S.

dollar, the value of your investment could decrease when converted back to dollars, even if the European stocks perform well.

9.Non-Diversification Risk: While mutual funds are generally diversified, some funds may focus heavily on a particular sector, region, or type of asset.
- *Example:* A mutual fund that invests only in the energy sector can be very risky. If oil prices plummet, the entire fund could take a significant hit.

10.Redemption Risk: Redemption risk is the risk that a mutual fund will have to sell investments at a bad time to meet shareholder redemptions (when investors want their money back).
- *Example:* During the 2008 financial crisis, many investors pulled their money out of mutual funds. Some funds had to sell assets at rock-bottom prices to meet these redemptions, hurting the remaining investors.

11. Regulatory Risk: Changes in laws and regulations can impact mutual funds and their performance.

•*Example*: If new tax laws are introduced that change how mutual funds are taxed, the value of your investment could be affected. Similarly, new regulations might restrict the types of investments a mutual fund can make.

12. Short-Term Performance Risk: It's important to remember that mutual fund performance can be volatile in the short term.

•*Example:* If you invest in a stock mutual fund, and there's a sudden market downturn, the value of your investment can drop significantly in a short period. If you need to withdraw your money during this downturn, you might have to sell at a loss.

Understanding the risks of mutual funds is very salient for making informed investment decisions. While mutual funds offer many advantages, it's important to be aware of the potential downsides. By knowing these risks, you can better assess whether a particular mutual fund fits your investment goals and risk tolerance.

CHAPTER 5.

ETFs - THE VERSATILE INVESTMENT VEHICLE

INTRODUCTION TO ETFs

Let me tell you about ETFs,(Exchange-Traded Funds). If what you want is a flexible and cost-effective way to invest, ETFs might just be the answer. They're kind of like a hybrid between mutual funds and individual stocks, offering some unique benefits. Let me break this down for you

What Are ETFs?

ETFs are investment funds that trade on stock exchanges, much like individual stocks. They hold a collection of assets, such as stocks, bonds, or other securities, and their main goal is to track the performance of a specific index, sector, commodity, or other assets.

HOW DO ETFs WORK?

Here's a basic rundown:

1. Structure: An ETF is created by a financial institution that buys a group of assets and puts them in a fund. Shares of this fund are then sold to investors.

2. Trading: You can buy and sell ETF shares on a stock exchange throughout the trading day, just like you would with individual stocks. This means you can take advantage of price changes during the day, unlike mutual funds, which only trade at the end of the trading day.

3. Diversification: When you buy shares of an ETF, you're essentially getting a slice of a diversified portfolio. This helps spread out your risk because the ETF holds a variety of assets.

TYPES OF ETFs

There are various types of ETFs, each serving different investment strategies:

1.Index ETFs: These track a specific index, like the S&P 500, allowing you to invest in a broad market segment with one purchase.

2.Sector and Industry ETFs: These focus on specific sectors or industries, like technology, healthcare, or energy. They're great if you want to target a particular part of the economy.

3.Bond ETFs: These invest in bonds, providing a way to get exposure to fixed-income securities with the flexibility of stock trading.

4.Commodity ETFs: These invest in physical commodities like gold, oil, or agricultural products. They're useful for investors looking to diversify into raw materials.

5.International ETFs: These give you exposure to markets outside your home country, helping you diversify globally.

6.Thematic ETFs: These focus on specific investment themes, like clean energy, artificial intelligence, or emerging markets.

HOW TO INVEST IN ETFS

Investing in ETFs is a smart way to build a diversified portfolio, and it's pretty straightforward. Here's how:

1.Open a Brokerage Account

First things first, you'll need a brokerage account to buy and sell ETFs. If you don't already have one, don't worry—it's easy to set up.

There are many online brokers like E*TRADE, Fidelity, TD Ameritrade, or Robinhood. Choose one that offers low fees and a user-friendly platform. Most brokers have simple signup processes where you'll provide some personal information and link your bank account.

2.Understand Your Investment Goals
Before you start buying ETFs, it's important to know what you're aiming for.
 If you are looking for long-term growth, regular income, or perhaps a way to balance your existing portfolio, Your goals will help determine which types of ETFs are right for you.

3.Do Your Research
There are thousands of ETFs out there, so you'll need to do some homework to find the best ones for your needs,what you need to do is look at the ETF's objective, the index it tracks, its expense ratio (the annual fee as a percentage of your investment), and its historical performance. Websites like Morningstar and ETF.com provide detailed information and comparisons.

4.Choose the Right ETFs

Based on your research and goals, select the ETFs that best match your investment strategy. Let me simplify it;If you want broad market exposure, you might choose an S&P 500 ETF like SPY or VOO. For sector-specific investments, consider something like XLK for technology or XLF for financials. If you're interested in bonds, look at BND for a diversified bond ETF.

5.Place Your Order

Now that you've chosen your ETFs, it's time to buy. You can do this by Logging into your brokerage account, enter the ticker symbol of the ETF you want to buy, and decide how many shares you want. You can place a market order (buying at the current price) or a limit order (setting a maximum price you're willing to pay).

6.Monitor Your Investments

Once you've bought your ETFs, keep an eye on how they're performing and how they fit into your overall portfolio.that is;you can check in on your investments regularly to see if they're meeting your goals. If the market shifts or your investment objectives change, you might need to rebalance your portfolio by buying or selling different ETFs.

7.Consider Dollar-Cost Averaging
If you're investing a fixed amount regularly, you can take advantage of dollar-cost averaging, which can reduce the impact of market volatility.An example is by Setting up automatic monthly investments into your chosen ETFs. This way, you buy more shares when prices are low and fewer when prices are high, potentially lowering your average cost per share over time.

8.Be Mindful of Fees
Even though ETFs typically have lower fees than mutual funds, it's still important to be aware of any costs involved,you have to watch

out for trading commissions, especially if you're making frequent trades. Some brokers offer commission-free ETFs, which can save you money.

9.Stay Informed
Markets and personal circumstances change, so staying informed is very important.
Keep up with market news, read investment analyses, and periodically review your financial goals. This will help you make informed decisions and adjust your portfolio as needed.

10.Rebalance Your Portfolio
Over time, the value of your ETFs may change, affecting your portfolio's asset allocation. Rebalancing helps maintain your desired risk level.
Hear this,If you wanted a 70% stocks and 30% bonds portfolio, but your stock ETFs have grown to make up 80% of your portfolio, you'd sell some stock ETFs and buy bond ETFs to get back to your original allocation.

Investing in ETFs is a fantastic way to build a diversified portfolio with flexibility and lower costs.you can confidently start your ETF investment journey by following the steps mentioned earlier.

ADVANTAGES AND DISADVANTAGES OF ETFS

ETFs (Exchange-Traded Funds)is a popular choice for many investors, but like anything, they come with their own set of advantages and disadvantages. Here's what you need to know.

ADVANTAGES OF ETFs

1.Diversification

When you buy a single ETF, you're getting exposure to a whole basket of assets. For instance, if you buy an S&P 500 ETF, you're effectively investing in 500 different companies. This spreads out your risk because your investment isn't tied to the performance of just one company.

2. Flexibility

ETFs trade on stock exchanges just like individual stocks. It being flexible means you can buy and sell them throughout the trading day at market prices. If you see an opportunity or need to make a quick move, ETFs give you that flexibility.

3. Lower Costs

ETFs typically have lower expense ratios compared to mutual funds because many ETFs are passively managed. For instance, an S&P 500 ETF just tracks the index and doesn't require active management, which keeps costs down.

4. Transparency

Most ETFs disclose their holdings daily, so you always know exactly what assets the ETF holds.

This transparency can help you make more informed and better investment decisions.

5. Tax Efficiency
ETFs are generally more tax-efficient than mutual funds. They have a unique structure that minimizes capital gains distributions, so you might end up with a lower tax bill compared to similar mutual fund investments.

DISADVANTAGES OF ETFS

1. Trading Costs
While ETFs generally have lower expense ratios, you may still incur trading costs every time you buy or sell ETF shares. If you're making frequent trades, these costs can add up, especially if your broker charges commissions.

2. Market Risk

Like any investment tied to the stock market, ETFs are subject to market risk. If the market takes a downturn, the value of your ETF can drop. For instance, during the 2008 financial crisis, many ETFs saw significant declines along with the overall market.

3. Complexity

While ETFs can be simple in concept, some types of ETFs—like leveraged or inverse ETFs—are more complex and carry higher risks. These are designed for more experienced investors and can behave in ways that may be unexpected for beginners.

4. Tracking Error

Although ETFs are designed to track an index, there can be slight discrepancies between the ETF's performance and the index's performance, known as tracking error. This can occur due to management fees, transaction costs, or other factors.

5. Dividend Reinvestment

Not all brokers offer automatic dividend reinvestment for ETFs. This means that if your ETF pays dividends, you might have to manually reinvest them, which can be less convenient compared to mutual funds that automatically reinvest dividends.

CONCLUSION

You have taken a very important move by educating yourself about investing. Now, it's time to put what you've learned into action. Start with a plan, make informed decisions, and remember that every investor, no matter how successful, was once a beginner. With patience, persistence, and the right strategies, you'll be well on your way to financial success and freedom.

Investing is a powerful tool for building wealth and achieving financial independence. By starting early, staying disciplined, and continuously learning, you're setting yourself up for a brighter financial future. It's natural to feel apprehensive at first, but the more you engage with the process, the more confident you'll become.

Think of your investments as seeds you're planting today to harvest in the future. With time, care, and patience, these seeds will grow and flourish, providing you with financial security and opportunities. Whether your goal is to retire comfortably, fund your children's education, or travel the world, smart investing can help you get there.

YOUR FREE GIFT.

BEST RESOURCES AND TOOLS FOR INVESTORS

Having the right resources and tools can make a huge difference. I will tell you some of the best ones out there that can help you make informed & concise decisions and keep track of your investments. Here's a rundown of some must-have tools and resources for investors.

1. Financial News Websites

Staying updated with the latest news is crucial for any investor. Here are some top websites to keep you in the loop:

- **Bloomberg:** Offers in-depth market analysis and financial news. Great for staying on top of global market trends.

- **Reuters:** Provides timely news on markets, companies, and economic events.
- **CNBC:** A go-to for live market updates and expert analysis.

Suppose there's news about a new regulation affecting the tech industry. Checking Bloomberg or CNBC can give you detailed insights and help you understand how it might impact your investments.

2. Investment Research Platforms

These platforms provide in-depth analysis and research reports:

- **Morningstar:** Known for its comprehensive research reports, ratings, and financial data. Ideal for fundamental analysis.
- **Value Line:** Offers detailed reports and ratings on stocks, making it a great resource for value investors.
- **Zacks Investment Research:** Provides stock rankings and research reports, helping you identify potential winners.

If you're considering investing in a new company, Morningstar can give you a detailed report on its financial health, historical performance, and future prospects.

3. Stock Screeners
Finding the right stocks to invest in can be challenging. Stock screeners help you filter through thousands of stocks based on specific criteria.

- **Finviz:** Excellent for both technical and fundamental screening. It offers a user-friendly interface and advanced filters.
- **Yahoo Finance:** Great for beginners with its simple and intuitive screening tools.
- **TradingView:** Provides advanced charting and technical analysis tools. Ideal for technical traders.

You want to find tech stocks with a P/E ratio below 20 and a market cap over $10 billion.

Using Finviz, you can quickly set these filters and get a list of matching stocks.

4. Portfolio Management Tools
Keeping track of your investments is essential. These tools can help you monitor your portfolio and make adjustments as needed:
- **Personal Capital:** A comprehensive financial management tool that tracks your investments, expenses, and net worth.
- **Mint:** While primarily a budgeting tool, Mint also offers features to track your investment portfolio.
- **Morningstar Portfolio Manager:** Allows you to track your investments and get detailed analysis on performance and asset allocation.

Personal Capital can show you how your portfolio is performing, help you understand your asset allocation, and even provide retirement planning advice.

5. Mobile Apps

For on-the-go investing, these mobile apps are incredibly handy:

- **Robinhood:** Commission-free trading with a user-friendly interface. Great for beginners.
- **E-TRADE:** Offers comprehensive trading tools and educational resources.
- **TD Ameritrade:** Provides powerful trading platforms like thinkorswim, which are great for both beginners and advanced traders.

If you're out and about and want to buy or sell stocks quickly, Robinhood's app makes it easy to execute trades right from your phone.

6. Educational Resources

Learning is a continuous process in investing. These resources can help you build your knowledge:

- **Investopedia:** A comprehensive resource for financial education, offering articles, tutorials, and a stock market simulator.

- **The Motley Fool:** Provides investment advice, stock picks, and educational content to help you make informed decisions.
- **Khan Academy:** Offers free courses on finance and economics, which can help you understand the fundamentals of investing.

If you're new to investing and want to understand how bonds work, Investopedia has detailed articles and tutorials that can explain everything in simple terms.

7. Financial Calculators

These tools can help you plan and make smarter financial decisions:

- **Bankrate:** Offers a variety of calculators, including retirement, mortgage, and investment calculators.
- **Investor.gov:** The SEC's website provides tools like the compound interest calculator and risk tolerance assessment.

- **Vanguard:** Their website features calculators for retirement planning, investment goals, and more.

Use the compound interest calculator on Investor.gov to see how your investments can grow over time with regular contributions and a certain interest rate.

One of the best tools you can use is a stock screener. Stock screeners help you filter through thousands of stocks based on specific criteria, making it easier to find potential investments that match your strategy.

Personally, I think *Finviz* offers a great balance of usability, advanced features, and visualization tools. It's particularly strong for both fundamental and technical screening, and the premium version is reasonably priced if you need real-time data and more advanced tools.

So **FINVIZ** is my favorite tool and here's why:

1.Visual Tools: Finviz provides powerful visualization tools like heat maps and charts.
2.Advanced Filters: You can screen for technical indicators, patterns, and more.
3.Free and Premium: The free version is robust, but the premium version offers real-time data and more advanced features.

- If you're interested in finding stocks that have recently hit new highs or lows, Finviz makes it easy with its technical filters and visual charts.

THE BEST TOOLS I HIGHLY RECOMMEND FOR A BEGINNER

As a Beginner in the world of investing, it can feel a bit overwhelming, but having the right tools can make a huge difference. Two of the best resources for beginners are Yahoo Finance and

Google Finance. Let's talk about why they're so great, Beginner friendly and how they can help you get started on your investment journey.

1. YAHOO FINANCE

Why It's Great for Beginners:

●.User-Friendly Interface
Yahoo Finance has a clean, easy-to-navigate layout. Even if you're new to investing, you'll find it straightforward to use. The homepage gives you a quick snapshot of the market, top news, and major indices.

●Comprehensive Data
You can look up any stock and get detailed information, including price history, financial statements, and analyst ratings. Let's say you're interested in Apple (AAPL). A quick search will give you a wealth of information, from historical price charts to financial performance data.

- **Customizable Watchlists**

You can create your own watchlists to track the stocks you're interested in. This is super handy for keeping an eye on your potential investments. If you're watching tech stocks, you can add them to your watchlist and get updates on their performance in one place.

- **News and Analysis**

Yahoo Finance aggregates news from various sources, giving you access to the latest articles and reports on the stocks and markets you care about. You can read expert opinions and stay informed about the factors influencing your investments.

- **Portfolio Management Tools**

You can set up a portfolio on Yahoo Finance to track your investments. It shows your gains and losses, helps you monitor your performance, and provides insights into your portfolio's health. This is great for keeping your investments organized.

2. GOOGLE FINANCE

Why It's Great for Beginners:

●Integration with Google Ecosystem
If you already use Google services like Gmail or Google Sheets, Google Finance integrates seamlessly. You can pull in financial data directly into your spreadsheets for analysis, making it easier to track and manage your investments.

●Simple and Intuitive
Google Finance is designed to be straightforward. The interface is clean, with no unnecessary clutter. This makes it perfect for beginners who want to focus on the essentials without getting overwhelmed.

●Real-Time Market Data

Google Finance provides real-time stock quotes and charts, so you're always up-to-date with the latest market movements. If you're tracking a particular stock, you can see its real-time price changes throughout the trading day.

- **Customizable Watchlists**

Similar to Yahoo Finance, Google Finance allows you to create watchlists. You can add stocks, track their performance, and get updates all in one place. This helps you stay organized and informed about the stocks you're interested in.

- **News Integration**

Google Finance pulls in news stories related to the stocks and sectors you're following. This means you can quickly catch up on the latest developments and understand how they might impact your investments.

Which One to Choose?

Both Yahoo Finance and Google Finance are excellent tools for beginners, and the best one for you depends on your preferences and needs.

●If you want a more comprehensive set of tools and detailed financial data, Yahoo Finance might be the better choice. It offers robust portfolio management features and extensive market analysis.

●If you prefer simplicity and seamless integration with other Google services, Google Finance is fantastic. It's easy to use and provides all the essential information without overwhelming you.

INVESTMENT STRATEGIES AND TIPS

Getting started with investing can seem a bit daunting, but don't worry—I've got some strategies and tips that will help you get on the right track. Think of this as our little chat about how to start investing smartly and confidently.

1. Start with a Plan

Why It is Important
- **Set Goals**: Before you invest, it's important to know what you're investing for. Are you saving for retirement, a down payment on a house, or maybe your kid's education?
- **Time Horizon:** Your investment strategy will depend a lot on how long you plan to invest. Longer time horizons can typically handle more risk.

Tip: If you're saving for retirement that's 30 years away, you can afford to take more risks compared to saving for a house you want to buy in five years.

2. Diversify Your Portfolio

Why It is Important
- **Reduce Risk:** Don't put all your eggs in one basket. By spreading your investments across different asset classes (stocks, bonds, real estate,

etc.), you reduce the risk of losing everything if one investment performs poorly.

Tip:Instead of investing all your money in tech stocks, you might also invest in bonds, international stocks, and maybe a bit of real estate.

3.Understand Your Risk Tolerance

Why It is Important

●**Comfort Level:** Knowing how much risk you're comfortable with will help you choose the right investments. If market fluctuations make you nervous, you might prefer more stable investments.

Tip: If you're conservative, you might favor bonds and dividend-paying stocks over high-growth tech stocks.

4.Do Your Research

Why It is Important

- **Informed Decisions:** Don't just invest in a company because everyone else is. Make sure you understand what you're investing in.

Tip: If you're considering buying stock in a company, look into its financial health, market position, and future growth prospects.

5. Consider Index Funds and ETFs

Why It is Important

- **Low Cost:** Index funds and ETFs typically have lower fees compared to actively managed funds.
- **Diversification:** They provide instant diversification because they track a broad market index.

Tip: Investing in an S&P 500 index fund means you're investing in 500 of the largest U.S. companies, which gives you broad market exposure.

6. Don't Try to Time the Market

Why It is Important

•**Consistency:** It's almost impossible to predict market highs and lows. Instead of trying to time the market, focus on consistent, regular investing.

Tip: Consider using dollar-cost averaging, where you invest a fixed amount regularly. This helps you buy more shares when prices are low and fewer when prices are high.

7. Keep an Eye on Fees

Why It is Important

•**Impact on Returns:** High fees can eat into your returns over time. Be mindful of expense ratios, transaction fees, and other costs associated with investing.

Tip: Compare the expense ratios of different mutual funds or ETFs before investing. Even a small difference can add up over the long term.

8. Rebalance Your Portfolio

Why It is Important

- **Maintain Allocation:** Over time, some investments will grow faster than others, which can throw your asset allocation out of balance. Regular rebalancing helps maintain your desired risk level.

Tip: If your target allocation is 60% stocks and 40% bonds, but your stocks have grown to 70%, you'll need to sell some stocks or buy more bonds to get back to your original allocation.

9. Stay Informed but Avoid Overreacting

Why It is Important

- **Long-Term Focus:** Markets can be volatile, but it's important to stay focused on your long-term goals and not make hasty decisions based on short-term market movements.

Tip: During market downturns, it's tempting to sell everything. But if your goals are long-term, it's usually better to stay the course and ride out the volatility.

10. Consider Working with a Financial Advisor

Why It is Important
- **Expert Guidance:** A financial advisor can help you create a personalized investment plan, choose the right investments, and stay on track to meet your goals.

Tip: If you're unsure about where to start or how to manage your portfolio, a financial advisor can provide valuable insights and support.

5 COMMON INVESTMENT MISTAKES AND HOW TO AVOID THEM AS A BEGINNER

Jumping into the world of investing is exciting, but it's also easy to make mistakes when you're just starting out. I'll tell you about some of the most common mistakes beginners make and how you can avoid them. This way, you'll be better prepared and more confident as you start your investing journey.

1.NOT HAVING A PLAN

Why It's a Mistake

- **Lack of Direction:** Investing without a plan is like driving without a map. You might end up somewhere, but it's probably not where you intended to go.
- **Emotional Decisions:** Without a plan, you're more likely to make decisions based on emotions rather than logic.

Imagine you start investing because you heard a hot stock tip. Without understanding your own financial goals or how this investment fits into them, you might end up with more risk than you're comfortable with.

How to Avoid Such Mistake

- **Set Clear Goals:** Determine what you're investing for (retirement, buying a house, etc.) and your time horizon.
- **Create a Strategy:** Based on your goals, develop an investment strategy that outlines what types of investments you'll make and how much risk you're willing to take.

2.FAILING TO DIVERSIFY

Why It's a Mistake

- **Increased Risk:** Putting all your money into one or a few investments increases your risk. If one investment tanks, your whole portfolio can suffer.

●**Missed Opportunities:** You might miss out on gains in other sectors or asset classes.

Investing all your money in a single tech stock might be great if the stock soars, but if it crashes, you could lose a significant portion of your investment.

How to Avoid Such Mistake

●**Spread Your Investments:** Diversify across different asset classes (stocks, bonds, real estate) and sectors (tech, healthcare, finance).

●**Use Funds:** Consider investing in mutual funds or ETFs, which provide instant diversification by pooling many investments together.

3.IGNORING FEES AND EXPENSES

Why It's a Mistake

- **Erodes Returns:** High fees and expenses can eat into your investment returns over time.
- **Compounded Costs:** Even small fees can add up significantly over the long term.

If you're paying a 1% management fee on your investments, it might not seem like much. But over 30 years, that 1% can make a huge difference in your total returns.

How to Avoid Such Mistake

- **Compare Fees:** Look at the expense ratios of mutual funds and ETFs before investing.
- **Opt for Low-Cost Options:** Consider low-cost index funds and ETFs, which typically have lower fees compared to actively managed funds.

4. TRYING TO TIME THE MARKET

Why It's a Mistake

- **Unpredictable Markets:** Markets are unpredictable, and even seasoned investors struggle to time the market correctly.
- **Missed Opportunities:** By trying to buy low and sell high, you might miss out on some of the best days in the market.

Selling your stocks during a market dip out of fear could mean missing the rebound, which often happens quickly and unexpectedly.

How to Avoid Such Mistake

- **Stick to a Plan:** Focus on your long-term investment strategy rather than short-term market movements.
- **Regular Investing:** Use dollar-cost averaging, where you invest a fixed amount regularly, regardless of market conditions.

5. LETTING EMOTIONS DRIVE DECISIONS

Why It's a Mistake

- **Poor Decisions:** Emotional investing often leads to buying high (out of greed) and selling low (out of fear).
- **Stress:** Constantly reacting to market fluctuations can be stressful and exhausting.

Hearing news about a market downturn might tempt you to sell off your investments in a panic, potentially locking in losses instead of riding out the volatility.

How to Avoid Such Mistake

- **Stay Informed:** Educate yourself about investing to build confidence in your decisions.
- **Automate:** Set up automatic investments to keep you disciplined and reduce the temptation to make emotional decisions.

Avoiding these common mistakes can set you up for success as you start your investing journey. Remember, investing is a marathon, not a sprint. By having a plan, diversifying your portfolio, being mindful of fees, avoiding market timing, and keeping your emotions in check, you'll be well on your way to building a solid financial future.

www.ingramcontent.com/pod-product-compliance
Lightning Source LLC
Chambersburg PA
CBHW071942210526
45479CB00002B/787